My Tears in a Bottle

Published by Kirk House Publishers
Burnsville, Minnesota

Kathy wrote this book dedicated to her son, Bryon, not to only bring healing to her own heart, but in time to help others in the midst of their own grief. She makes it known that her faith is real and that her trust in God has brought her to a life that is not the same as before, but life can once again be complete and meaningful.

~**Wendy Puckett, Kathy's Sister**

Although death is an inevitable part of life, we cling to control and security. In this book my close friend, Kathy, articulates her personal struggle after her son's sudden death. She shares with refreshing honesty about her raw grief. *My Tears in a Bottle* is a reminder that our current reality is not our final reality, and God is Lord over all pain and suffering. If you long for peace and healing, I highly recommend this book.

~**Karen Ernst, Friend and Prayer Partner**

My Tears in a Bottle, A Mother's Journey of Grief and Healing, written by Kathy Allen, is a beautiful story of God's amazing grace in healing deep wounds. While life is wonderful, it is also hard and unpredictable. Kathy faces one of the hardest trials, the death of her son. Walk with her as she reminisces back to that terrible day and shares how God used every hurt, tear, emotion and thought for His glory. He walked alongside Kathy and healed her from the inside out. She now walks alongside others in their grief and helps them to find healing.

~**Carol German, Friend and Author of** *God Hears My Heart*

Kathy has shared her story of grief and healing in such a way that you are drawn into the account, and are able to experience the journey with her.

~**Pastor Art Hansen, Care Pastor/GriefShare Ministry, Friendship Church**

A MOTHER'S JOURNEY OF GRIEF AND HEALING

My Tears in a Bottle

KATHY PUCKETT ALLEN

My Tears in a Bottle: A Mother's Journey of Grief and Healing
© Copyright 2021 Kathy Puckett Allen

All rights reserved. No part of this book may be used or reproduced in any manner whatsoever without written permission of the author except in the case of brief quotations embodied in critical articles and reviews.

The information in this book is distributed as an "as is" basis, without warranty. Although every precaution has been taken in the preparation of this work, neither the author nor the publisher shall have any liability to any person or entity with respect to any loss or damage caused or alleged to be caused directly or indirectly by the information contained in this book.

First Edition
ISBN: 9781952976209
Library of Congress Control Number: 2021911308

Cover Design: Mary Solverson

Published by Kirk House Publishers
1250 E 115th Street
Burnsville, MN 55337
Kirkhousepublishers.com
612-781-2815

Dedication

My book, *My Tears in a Bottle: A Mother's Journey of Grief and Healing*, is dedicated to the memory of my son Bryon A. Allen. Thank you, Bryon, for your gift of a small, black notebook with pages you unwittingly left blank—so that your mother, when she found it, would begin to fill the notebook with words.

These words would ultimately bring God's healing to this mother's shattered and broken heart. As hope began to rise within me, I knew definitively that my son's death would not be in vain, for a book had been conceived in my heart, and I recognized that one day it would be published.

As the psalmist David also wrote: "I am recording this so that future generations will also praise the Lord for all that He has done." — Psalms 102:18

*"You keep track of all my sorrows.
You have collected all my tears in your bottle.
You have recorded each one in your book."*
— Psalm 56:8

Acknowledgments

I acknowledge and bestow all the glory and honor to God, for without Him, *My Tears in a Bottle* would never have been written. It was God who placed such a deep desire within my heart to write about my son Bryon, who tragically died in a car accident in 1993. I must state that "He (God) has given me a new song to sing, of praises to our God. Now many will hear of the glorious things he did for me, and stand in awe before the Lord, and put their trust in him." — Psalm 40:3.

I acknowledge my husband, Roger, who walked faithfully with me through the journey of grief and healing. He encouraged me to write the story of our son's death, even though he did not understand how I could put it all into words.

I acknowledge my son Bruce—ever patient with me when I asked him to take pictures of Bryon's grave marker at Mount Pleasant Cemetery. I have faith, Bruce, in the belief that you are proud of your mother as she wrote and dedicated her book to the memory of your brother, Bryon.

I acknowledge Mary Solverson. There are no words to express my gratitude for this book's beautifully illustrated cover.

I acknowledge my church family, who relentlessly prayed, cried, supported, and encouraged my family and me during the most difficult period in our lives. Their unconditional love truly expressed the love of Jesus.

I acknowledge those who read the first version of my book and gave their valuable input:

1. Bruce Allen
2. Colette Allen
3. Roger Allen
4. Sharon Cowhey
5. Karen Ernst
6. Carol German
7. Pastor Art Hansen
8. Laura Puckett
9. Tim Puckett
10. Wendy Puckett
11. Mary Solverson

And professionally, Connie Anderson, Editor, Words & Deeds, Inc., and Ann Aubitz, Publisher, Kirk House Publishers, gave me invaluable insights and suggestions.

Table of Contents

Chapter 1	**Let the Writing Begin**	**13**
Chapter 2	Remembering the Good Times	17
Chapter 3	Devastating News	23
Chapter 4	A Death has Occurred	31
Chapter 5	Calling Our Son, Bruce	35
Chapter 6	Bryon's Body Comes Home	39
Chapter 7	Military Funeral Preparations	43
Chapter 8	The Morning of the Funeral	49
Chapter 9	Military Funeral	55
Chapter 10	The U.S. Army Transport Truck Arrives	63
Chapter 11	The Containers	67
Chapter 12	The Small Black Notebook	71
Chapter 13	Bryon, The Soldier	75
Chapter 14	Bryon, The Person	79

Chapter 15	Look Out, Kathy is on a Mission	85
Chapter 16	That Day, as Told by Bruce	91
Chapter 17	The Leather Baseball Glove, as Told by Dad	99
Chapter 18	The Three Yellow Roses	107
Chapter 19	The Grieving Blanket	111
Chapter 20	My Dream of Writing a Book	115
Chapter 21	Through It All: God's Healing	119
Chapter 22	Jerky, Anyone	125
Chapter 23	What We Have Lost	129
Chapter 24	Griefshare Ministry	133
Chapter 25	What Not to Say	139
Chapter 26	Additional Pictures	143
Chapter 27	My Personal Testimony	151
	Tribute to Service Members	153
	About the Author	155

Chapter 1
Let the Writing Begin

"The righteous cry out, and the Lord hears them."
— Psalms 34:17

But, nevertheless, I could not escape the fact that a death had occurred, and though I did not want to, I felt compelled to relive and write about that ill-fated day.

It was January 1994 and as I sat at my kitchen table, I was anxious and reluctant to write down the words that were in my heart. My hand shook uncontrollably, and I thought, "How can I write when my hand is trembling so much that I cannot even hold the pen?" I laid down the pen, lowered my head, and prayed, "Lord, if I am to write what I so desperately want to articulate, please help to calm these unsteady hands." I took a deep breath, and after a short while, I was able to place my pen on the first blank page of my son Bryon's small, black military logbook. And slowly, I began to express with words what I so urgently wanted to write.

I wrote and wrote in that logbook. Words poured out to God about my aching and shattered heart—I *could not* stop the flow. I wrote that most days, I felt as though I would go mad from the unrelenting, merciless thoughts regarding the death of my son. These thoughts were trapped within my mind, and there was no escape from them. They were with me constantly—unrelenting and never ceasing. Even when I attempted to escape through sleep, the thoughts of his death were unyielding. I simply wanted the insanity to end. "I will lie down in peace and sleep, for you alone, O Lord, will keep me safe" — Psalms 4:8. As I read and committed this scripture to memory, I discovered that after several weeks, I was able to lie down in peace and sleep the night through. Blessed, peaceful sleep. Thank you, Lord that you heard and answered my prayer.

But, nevertheless, I could not escape the fact that a death had occurred, and though I did not want to, I felt compelled to relive and write about that ill-fated day, Sunday, August 29, 1993. I longed to write down what had occurred on that day. As painful as it would be to put in writing the events that led up to Bryon's death, I felt an urgency to write down the specifics. My expectation was that perhaps if I relived the tragic death of my son, there might be a ray of hope that my heart would in time be restored and made whole again. For this reason, I needed to tell the story in order that others might also know what happened on the day of Bryon's death—to prayerfully bring closure and healing to all who knew and loved Bryon as a son, a brother, a grandson, a cousin, a nephew, a friend, and a comrade.

I again prayed and asked the Lord for help. "The righteous cry out, and the Lord hears them." — Psalms 34:17

Chapter 2
Remembering the Good Times

"Enter into His gates with thanksgiving, and into His courts with praise. Be thankful to Him and bless His name."
— Psalm 100:4

My concluding words to him that night were to be safe the last miles of his trip and to call us collect on Sunday night to let us know of his safe arrival. Bryon told us that he would be certain to call when he reached his barracks.

That call never came.

Monday, August 30, 1993, a few minutes past 6:00 a.m.—a time that would forever be etched into our family's minds, as you, the reader, will soon learn.

My husband, Roger, and I were in our car, driving to the truck terminal where he was employed. I recall that I enjoyed the stillness and the quiet of that morning before rush-hour traffic—"the calm before the storm," as the saying goes. We were both decidedly quiet in the car. No need for conversation. In all likelihood, we were thinking about our two young sons, Bryon and Bruce, who unwittingly left us at the same time. Bryon, age twenty, had reenlisted for another three years in the U.S. Army. His brother Bruce, age eighteen, had decided to follow in his brother's footsteps and had also enlisted in the U.S. Army.

One after the other, our sons set out on new adventures. Bruce left on August 20 for basic training at Fort Sill, Oklahoma. A week later, on Saturday morning, August 28, after packing his 1989 Ford Escort full up and then some, Bryon left for Fort Bragg, North Carolina, where he was a print company armorer and supply specialist, as well as a member of the Psychological Operations Dissemination Battalion (Airborne). He had reenlisted for another three-year term with the army. Bryon enjoyed the discipline of army life and the benefits that the army offered him, which included a college education in criminal justice.

As we continued on our quiet drive, I reflected on the events of the past month when Bryon had been home on his military leave. I smiled as I visualized Bryon washing and waxing his car in our driveway. He worked hard to keep his first car spotless and shiny. I recalled that he took time to visit friends and family who he had not seen in many months. Bryon enjoyed the food that we cooked on our outside barbeque grill most every night. He stated that he could not get enough home-cooked meals because he would soon once again be eating at the mess hall, where, he maintained, the food was definitely not like his mom's home-cooked meals. Bryon devotedly continued his army physical training while home. He pumped iron, and he ran several miles every day. Bryon's two-week army leave turned into thirty days. He had wanted to spend more time with his family and friends. The extra two weeks with our son were a blessing from God that we will never forget. "And God is able to bless you abundantly." — 2 Corinthians 9:8a

I thought fondly of our two sons, Bryon and Bruce, as they spent quality time together as brothers. There was a need for them to become reacquainted after two years' separation. And Bryon, of course, enlightened his younger brother about military life and what he could expect. Bryon also spent a lot of time with his eight-year-old foster brother, Steven. "Thank you, Lord," I prayed silently to myself. "Thank you for the past month of special memories. Even though I miss my sons and my heart is sad, I am grateful for the time we had together as a family."

Once again, I thought fondly of Bryon. I could not help but smile to myself as I observed his car jam-packed full of the essential items that he would need back at Fort Bragg. I remembered his smile as he drove away and waved at his parents through the open window of his car. Unbeknownst to us at that time, it was to be his *final goodbye wave*.

Bryon had planned to stop at his Uncle Tim's (my brother's) home in Indianapolis, Indiana, on Saturday night. After a good night's rest, he would continue the remainder of his trip on Sunday and arrive at Fort Bragg in the early evening. On Saturday night at around ten, my husband and I called Bryon to make sure that he had arrived safely at my brother's home. My concluding words to him that night were to be safe the last miles of his trip and to call us collect on Sunday night to let us know of his safe arrival. Bryon told us that he would be certain to call when he reached his barracks. *That call never came.*

Brothers, Bryon and Bruce - 1993

Bryon with foster brother, Steven -1993

Chapter 3
Devastating News

"Hear my prayer, O Lord, listen to my cry for help,
Be not deaf to my weeping."
— Psalm 39:12

Dealing with his own immense shock, my husband made every effort to protect me. I could not breathe, my body was rigid, and I could not move—my mind was reeling from what I had just heard on the radio.

As Roger and I continued driving, I mulled over the fact that we had not heard from Bryon. He had not called us collect on Sunday evening, August 29. "That is so out of the ordinary," I reasoned. "It is not like Bryon to not have called, nor did he leave us a message on our answering machine to inform us that he had arrived safely. He is predictably dependable and mindful." I lightheartedly told my husband that night that I would have to take Bryon to task on Monday morning for not calling us. Nonetheless, why hadn't he called? I got a strange feeling in the pit of my stomach that I could not explain. I could not explain the uneasiness that I felt, but as a mother, I knew that something was definitely not right. I began to think over and over, "Why hasn't Bryon called? Why hasn't he called?"

I came back from my anxious thoughts. I needed a distraction, so I turned on the radio, which was tuned to our local news station. My decision to turn on the radio at that precise moment was about to take me and my husband into a state of unbelievable shock, pain, and devastation. God knew how our hearts would be broken, and He knew the pain we were about to suffer. God knew. At approximately 6:15 a.m., Roger and I heard the following heartbreaking words: "A twenty-year-old soldier from Chaska, Minnesota, was killed in an automobile accident yesterday, August 29, 1993, in Indianapolis, Indiana. His name was Bryon Albert."

I screamed out loud as I grabbed onto my seat for support. "No, please, God—this cannot be our son." "His name is *Bryon Albert Allen* not Bryon Albert."

Roger struggled to maintain control of the car. At the same time, he leaned over and grabbed my arm. In his own immense shock, my husband made every effort to protect me. I could not breathe, my body was rigid, and I could not move; my mind was reeling from what I had just heard on the radio. My mind could not grasp this horrific news—and it was whirling with questions. I screamed, "Why, how, when, where? Please, God, I begged. Do not let this news be true! Do not let it be our son Bryon."

Roger and I were in unspeakable shock, but our God—our protector—was in control of the situation. We were less than five minutes away from the home of Roger's aunt. I do not remember how—except with the help of God and his protecting angels—we were able to drive to her home without getting into a car accident ourselves. As we pulled into the driveway, his aunt stood at her front door, and I am sure that she wondered why we were there so early on a Monday morning. As Roger helped me out of the car, he had to all but carry me as my legs would not hold me up. I was extremely weak and in shock from the devastating news that we had just heard. His aunt quickly opened the front door and asked, "What is wrong? Has something happened?" She would soon learn, as we had, that something horrible indeed had happened.

Once inside her home, we shared the devastating news that we had heard about Bryon on the radio. Then we asked her if she had the morning newspaper. We were desperate to know if what we had heard on the radio was, in fact, true. We needed to know specifics. We needed answers. Yet even before we read the newspaper, we both knew in our hearts that what we had heard was true. But still, we needed proof—and that proof would be in the spelling of my son's first name: *Bryon*. As Roger and I opened the newspaper, fear and trepidation filled our hearts. Our hands trembled, and we were unable to concentrate on the task at hand. Roger's aunt calmly took the newspaper from us, and after she glanced hastily through the various articles, she located what we were looking for, and she read the following headline to us: "Soldier from Chaska Dies in Automobile Crash." The article continued, "A twenty-year-old soldier, Bryon Albert, died Sunday afternoon in a car accident in Indianapolis, Indiana. Paperwork in Albert's car indicated that he was traveling to Fort Bragg, North Carolina."

Correct first name and spelling, correct middle name, but no last name given. How could this horrible news be happening to us? My mind was spinning, I could not comprehend what I had heard on the radio, nor could

I comprehend what a moment ago was read from the newspaper. I took the newspaper from Roger's aunt to read for myself the spelling of my son's name. But before I read, I prayed silently, "Please, God, please let his name be misspelled or maybe even be another name. Don't let the name be my Bryon." But God did not answer my prayer as I thought He ought to have. As I opened my eyes, the name I read on the page was *Bryon Albert*. It was an unusual spelling for his name, but now I also knew it was my son. It was the correct first name and spelling and the correct middle name, but no last name was given. The information verified that our precious son Bryon had been killed.

It was incorrect information but enough for me to know in my heart that the information was accurate. "What happened?" I asked myself. I was so bewildered by everything that had taken place in the last hour. I remember that I had talked with Bryon on Saturday night when I had asked him to be cautious and drive safely. He had told me that he would. Why hadn't he listened?

"Please, God," I prayed, "What happened to cause my son's death? Please, God, let this all be a horrible nightmare." I had too many questions, and at this point, there were no tangible answers. The only tangible was that my son was dead. Killed in an automobile accident somewhere in Indianapolis, Indiana.

I grabbed my stomach and felt as though I would be sick. Roger's aunt gave me a glass of water and told me to sit down. But I did not want to sit down. I paced the floor. As I walked up and down, I recalled again that I had specifically told Bryon to be careful. He had told his mother that he would be careful. I screamed in my head, "Why didn't Bryon listen to me?! Oh, why wasn't he careful?!" I could not—would not—accept my son's death. What had really happened? "Please, God," I prayed, "Let this all be a horrible nightmare." My mind was not capable of comprehending such horrific news.

I prayed to myself that the news we had heard on the radio and read in the newspaper was a dreadful mistake. A possible mix-up of information. How could this news be true when no one from the army had notified us of our son's alleged death? No one had confirmed our son's death to us. I had too many questions, and at this juncture in time—there were just no concrete answers. The only tangible was that my son was apparently dead! My mind reeled, and my head ached. Our world had just been turned upside-down. There was no sense to be made. Only disbelief and confusion.

Roger and I stood in his aunt's living room. We were in unimaginably intense shock. We could not grasp or come to grips with the horrific news. We were completely numb, and we walked around in a state of confusion and bewilderment. We did not know what to do. We stared at one other, and the pain that we saw in each other's eyes was more than a husband or a wife should see in the other. We made an effort to hold and comfort one another, but the numbness we each felt could not bring consolation to either of us.

During the time we were at Roger's aunt's home, we were notified that an official from the army would be coming to our home to officially notify us of Bryon's death. So I have the "apparently dead" would soon turn into "officially dead." Officially dead. What did that mean anyway? Up until approximately three hours ago, we had thought that we had a son who was alive, and now we had found out that we had a son who was dead. We wanted to believe that there was still a possibility that a blunder had been made and that Bryon, in all actuality, was still alive. But our hearts told us differently. We knew the truth in our hearts. Our minds could not grasp what had transpired between when Bryon left on Saturday morning and his death at some time on Sunday. There were too many unanswered questions that we did not want to know the answers to. Oh, God in heaven, we did not want to know.

After we communicated the devastating news to our employers, it was time for us to leave and go home to await the arrival of the army official who would officially communicate to us the news of our beloved son's death.

Roger's aunt decided to ride with us so that she could look after us in our time of shock and disbelief. We knew that once we were home, we would have to make many phone calls to our loved ones, including to our son Bruce, who was in basic training.

"God help us," was all that I could manage to pray. "The righteous cry out, and the Lord hears, and delivers them out of all their troubles." — Psalm 34:17

Chapter 4
A Death Has Occurred

"My flesh and my heart may fail, but God is the strength of my heart and my portion forever."
— Psalm 73:26

The account of Bryon's death in Indianapolis was not only broadcast on the radio but was also printed in the newspapers.

At approximately 10:30 a.m. on Monday, August 30, 1993, the casualty assistance officer (CAO) from the United States Army arrived at our home and conveyed the official news of our son Bryon's death in Indiana. The CAO informed us that he had died at approximately 12:20 p.m. on Sunday, August 29, 1993, in a car accident on I-74 and Post Road, Marion County, Indianapolis. His death had been instantaneous. No one had knowledge of how he had lost control of his car, crossed over the median, and been struck broadside and ejected from his car. There were no witnesses. Bryon had left his Uncle Tim's home only one hour before his death. To this day, the accident and Bryon's death have remained a mystery. (Bryon was not wearing the lap belt in his car that would have given him the added protection he needed. His shoulder harness was intact, but when the door opened, the harness let loose, and Bryon was ejected and subsequently killed.)

The account of Bryon's death in Indianapolis was not only broadcast on the radio but also printed in the newspapers. We did not know how the Associated Press (AP) was able to uncover the information that surrounded our son's death and why it was allowed to be publicized without the army first notifying his parents. However, since Bryon's death, we have discovered that mistakes happen in this life. Regardless of whether we heard about his death on the radio, read about it in the newspaper, or heard the news officially from the army CAO at our home, Bryon was still deceased—and that fact would never change.

The hours and days that followed our son's death were a whirlwind of activity. I do not remember most of what transpired once we arrived home. So many details needed attention, but I was a mother in shock. I went through the motions of activities, but there was no emotion. For whatever reason, at the time, I was not able to cry—at least not right away. In due time, my tears would come, and when they did, those tears would be like a dam releasing its floodwaters.

Roger and I stood together in our garage in shock and utter disbelief, not knowing what to do. Roger later shared that as he stood in the garage, he had observed people, cars, and bicycles passing by. He had wanted to scream, "What is the matter with all of you people? Don't you know that our son is dead and we are in shock?" Then he prayed, "God help us all."

I do have a vivid recollection of a friend of ours who came to our home while we were both in the garage, not knowing what to do with ourselves. We heard our friend before we actually saw him. He came to us with wide-open arms as he wailed and sobbed at the news of Bryon's death. He took us in his arms and held us close. He sobbed and wept the tears that we ourselves could not cry. We will by no means forget this gesture of love from our friend who cried the tears that we could not cry for ourselves. Our pain was too great, too all-consuming.

"Blessed are those who mourn, for they will be comforted." — Matthew 5:4

Chapter 5
Calling Our Son, Bruce

*"Hear my prayer, O Lord, listen to my cry for help;
be not deaf to my weeping."*
— Psalm 39:12

Bruce shared that he did not believe it when he was told that his brother, Bryon, had been killed in a car accident. "That was the furthest thing from my mind," he relayed to us.

The hardest undertaking after learning of Bryon's death was to call our son, Bruce, who was in basic training at the time. Roger did not want another person to relay to

Bruce the shocking news about his brother's death. This difficult telephone call had to come from his dad, not through the newspaper or the radio. Absolutely no words described the anguish we felt as we heard Bruce scream over the phone, "No, no!" "It's not true. Please tell me it's not true. Bryon can't be dead!" After that, I do not remember anything more of the conversation between dad and son. I imagine it had to do with making arrangements for Bruce's flight home. I remember that I prayed for the Lord to please bring my young son home safely. I could not bear another loss.

Later, Bruce shared that when he had received the message about an important telephone call, he thought that something terrible had happened to his mother or his dad. He shared that he had not believed that his brother, Bryon, had been killed in a car accident. "That was the furthest thing from my mind," he relayed to us.

On Tuesday, August 31, Bruce arrived at the airport from Fort Sill, Oklahoma. We were there to meet him. I have no remembrance if it was a morning or afternoon flight. The time does not matter. What mattered was that we were there for our son, who was also in shock from the news of his brother's death. Our parental instincts dictated that we ought to console and comfort our son. Every fiber of our being wanted to protect and console our young son from the grief and pain he was suffering, but we knew that we could not. We ourselves needed to be consoled and comforted. I prayed silently to the Lord and asked, "What will happen to us? The pain in our hearts is so intense that I do not know how we will be able to bear under it. In your mercy, Lord, console and comfort us."

That night, as Roger and I lay in our bed, we made an effort to shut down our minds and tried not to think about the horrific events that had transpired since the early morning hours. We were in such a state of shock that as much as we wanted to, we could not understand nor comprehend the events that had taken place. "How could our son be dead?" we whispered to each other. "This has got to be a nightmare that we will soon awaken from. Please, dear God, let it be a nightmare."

We wanted to pray together, but we could barely speak in audible voices. Our bodies were weak from the shock of Bryon's death. Finally, we made an effort to pray. As I lay in my husband's arms, in a raspy whisper, Roger prayed, "Please, God, we are so afraid. The pain we feel is nearly unbearable. Please, God, in your mercy, hold Kathy and me in your loving arms. We are afraid, and we need you to hold us in your strong and loving arms. Thank you, God. Amen."

Neither Roger nor I slept that night. As much as we wanted to get the rest we so desired and needed, our minds would not shut off the events of the previous day.

As hard as I tried, my mind would not stay quiet. I so desperately wanted to cry, to scream, to shout, to shake my fist at God—to do something, anything, to release what was inside of me. But I could not; all I could do was lay there in my pain. All that was left now was a large, gaping wound in my heart that would take a very long time to heal. A very long time.

"Hear my prayer, O Lord, listen to my cry for help; be not deaf to my weeping." — Psalm 39:12

Chapter 6
Bryon's Body Comes Home

"For this God is our God for ever and ever: He will be our guide even unto death."
—Psalm 48:14

Bryon was not vibrant, nor was he alive. He was cold to the touch. I was in utter disbelief, and I was not able to comprehend the horrible death of my young son.

Bryon's body arrived home to his final resting place on the evening of Wednesday, September 1, 1993. My brother, Tim, who was a lieutenant commander in the navy and stationed in Indianapolis at the time of Bryon's death, escorted our son's body home. Even though Tim was in the navy and Bryon in the army, Tim was incredibly instrumental in conducting and managing all the aspects that pertained to Bryon's death in Indianapolis. And, because Tim was Bryon's uncle and nearest living relative at the time, the army authorities felt it was in the best interest of all concerned that he handle the many ensuing details of bringing Bryon's body back to Minnesota.

It would not be until many years later that I had the courage to ask Tim if he had been the one who had identified Bryon's body at the morgue in Indianapolis. "Yes," he responded. "And it was extremely difficult for me to view and identify the body of my nephew. I was reeling in shock myself, not believing that I had just seen Bryon the day before as he left for Fort Bragg. And now I was going to the morgue to confirm and identify the body of my nephew." Tim told me that going to the morgue to view Bryon's body caused him much angst.

Later that night after delivering Bryon's body to the funeral home, while awaiting arrangements, Tim came to our home. I thought about how distinguished he looked in his white dress navy uniform. Somehow it comforted me to know that Tim had been there with Bryon on the flight home to Minnesota. Two exceptionally proud military men in their uniforms. One military man to escort the deceased soldier home. The other military man, deceased and our son—a man who had proudly and willingly served and given his life in service for his country, the United States of America.

Tim Puckett, Lieutenant Commander, escorted Bryon's body home

The funeral home told us that immediate family members would be able to view Bryon's body at noon on Thursday, September 2. I do not recall a great deal about viewing my son's body for the first time. The memory is hazy and blurred. I remember, however, that I stood alongside my husband and held his hand. I was apprehensive, at first, to look at the body of my young son—apprehensive because I knew that this would be one of the last times I would see him. As I stood there, I thought how handsome he had looked in his army uniform, decorated with several merit medals. I saw that he held his airborne beret in his hand—the beret he had worn with pride. I approached the coffin cautiously, then I touched his fine-looking red hair and found that it was soft to the touch. But my once vibrant son did not move, nor did he respond to the touch of his grief-stricken mother. Bryon was not vibrant, nor was he alive. He was cold to the touch.

I was in utter disbelief, and I was not able to comprehend the horrible death of my young son. There were no tears (yet), just numbness, bewilderment, and confusion. It was difficult to leave our son at that place, but we, as Bryon's parents, had a military funeral to plan that would bring the respect and the honor due him. It would be one more final goodbye.

As I conclude this chapter, I am compelled to say "thank you" to Tim for being an advocate for our son. You took care of the innumerable, intricate details that needed to be completed before Bryon's body could come home to his final resting place. Thank you, Tim, from our entire family.

Chapter 7
Military Funeral Preparations

"In my Father's house are many mansions; if it were not so, I would have told you. I go to prepare a place for you."
— John 14:2

Wendy also shared with me that it had been extremely difficult for her to observe the soldiers practice their steps and formation in preparation for her nephew's funeral. She stated that she had also been in shock and that seeing those soldiers in her yard had almost been more than she could endure.

In all honesty, I do not remember a lot about the preparations for Bryon's funeral; my memory is fuzzy and unclear about many of the details. But I will relate what I do recall and what other people have recounted to me.

The day before Bryon's funeral, Roger and I were notified that there would be seven soldiers coming from Fort Bragg, North Carolina, to take part in Bryon's funeral. We were made aware that Bryon was well-respected and well-regarded by his fellow comrades. In retrospect, we also discovered that there were quite a number of soldiers who had volunteered to be casket bearers at Bryon's funeral, but only seven were chosen. So it was with great pride that we welcomed these seven soldiers to Minnesota to take part in our son's funeral.

A memorial service for Bryon was held at Fort Bragg on Thursday, September 2, so we expected that the army would no longer be involved with other details of Bryon's funeral. Not true. The army wanted very much to be involved in our son's funeral. We were overwhelmed and honored by this gesture. At the same time, Roger and I were very proud that both our sons had chosen to serve our country by joining the army (Roger also served in the army from 1967 to 1969). Regrettably, our eldest son, Bryon, died while he was in service for his country.

Roger and I were informed by Tim that normally, an army senior non-commissioned officer (NCO) or an officer would lead and perform the military funeral; however, it was agreed that Tim would be the officer-in-charge of Bryon's funeral. Even though Tim was in the navy stationed in Indianapolis, he was very instrumental in that he took care of all the minuscule details which related to Bryon's death and communicated with individuals at Fort Bragg. For example, Bryon was killed in Indianapolis, where Tim and his family lived. Tim identified Bryon's body. Tim dealt with the army and the many details surrounding Bryon's death, and, finally, Tim escorted Bryon's body home, military-style. Who better than my brother to take charge of an honorable military funeral?

On Friday morning, the day of the funeral, Tim met with the seven soldiers from Fort Bragg to practice their formation and steps. These brave, young soldiers wanted everything to be perfect for their comrade. It was not until several years later that I learned these soldiers had met at the home of my sister, Wendy, to practice outdoors in her backyard. She related to me that she had extended Minnesota hospitality by offering them refreshments, but they had politely declined because they had a lot to do in preparation for the two o'clock funeral service on Friday. Wendy also shared with me that it had been extremely difficult for her to observe the soldiers practice their steps and formation in preparation for her nephew's funeral. She stated that she had also been in shock and that seeing those soldiers in her yard had almost been more than she could endure. "I felt pride and shock," she told me. "Pride that Bryon had served his country by enlisting in the army. Shock that Bryon's fellow comrades had to come to Minnesota to do a military funeral to express their final farewells."

Not to be left out of the plans for the military funeral was my son, Bruce. In every sense, he wanted to be a part of paying his final respects to his brother. However, in view of the fact that Bruce had only been in the army nine days, he had not yet been issued his dress uniform. He needed a uniform and without delay. So, my brother, Tim, proceeded to Fort Snelling to make the acquisition. Tim was able to locate a dress uniform that he hoped would fit Bruce and brought it home. However, when Bruce tried the uniform on, it was far too large and needed a great deal of alterations. Fortunately, we knew of a local shop in the area that was well-known for their excellent alterations and modifications of garments. Tim and Bruce took the uniform to the shop and explained the tragic circumstances and that the uniform needed to be altered quickly and without delay for the funeral on Friday afternoon. The individuals at the shop promised they would do their best to have it ready by Friday morning, and true to their word, the uniform was ready to be picked up on Friday morning.

Friday morning, Bruce joined Tim and the soldiers from Fort Bragg at Wendy's home to practice for his brother's funeral. It was decided that Bruce would be the casket bearer or the guardian of the casket. This meant that during the funeral, Bruce would stand at attention by his brother's casket, signifying Bruce's final reverent tribute to his brother. The plan was that if at any particular time in the service, Bruce felt he could no longer stand at attention, he would quietly signal with a nod of his head that he needed to sit down. Bruce and another soldier would quietly pass each other and take their new positions. To the best of the military's ability, all scenarios were being taken into account so that Bryon's funeral would provide the respect and veneration due him.

Chapter 8
The Morning of the Funeral

*"Yea though I walk through the valley of the shadow of death,
I will fear no evil; for you are with me;
Your rod and Your staff, they comfort me."*
— Psalm 23:4

Again, in my mind, I screamed at God, "This is all nonsense, this is all madness! God, where were you when Bryon needed you? You could have protected him from that horrible accident—the accident that killed him. Why didn't you?!"

September 3, 1993—although it was painful and heart-wrenching, I was compelled to remember as much as possible about the events taking place on the day of Bryon's funeral. I was on an "important mission" to get the story written, and so through a veil of tears, I persevered. How, without God's help and intervention, would I ever be able to write this part of the book? Even now, after all these many years, it seems like only yesterday that my son died and I had a funeral to attend. And to again relive it today and put into words the events of his funeral makes my heart ache more than words can say. My tears had blinded me so that I could scarcely see the paper, yet I persevered on my mission. Whenever I struggled with my fragile emotions or grappled to find the right words to convey what was in my heart, I would pray and then wait on the Lord to help me. And again, God did not fail me.

Once more, God listened and heard my cry. "I waited patiently for God to help me, and he turned to me and heard my cry." — Psalm 40:1

Bryon's funeral was to be at 2:00 p.m., and that morning, as I recall, was a whirlwind of activity. More visitors stopped by our home to give their condolences. That, in turn, necessitated that an effort be made to be hospitable (at least in my own mind I thought so). I am confident that I was gracious to these visitors but the memory of it, truth be told, simply is not there. There were, however, enough family, friends, and neighbors to take care of the additional people gathered at our home. I just wandered around the house in a state of shock and disbelief or sat on our living room sofa with my hands folded in my lap, starring out of the window, devoid of any kind of emotion. Where my husband was, I do not know, but he was in all likelihood in the garage. That seemed to be his place of solace, his place to be alone with his grief and his sorrow. We each had our places where we went when we needed to be alone—whether in the house or in the garage, it did not matter. Bruce was with the soldiers from Fort Bragg practicing for his brother's funeral.

    Bryon was dead, and we all had much grief, much sorrow, and much pain in our hearts. Our emotions were fragile. The pain we were all dealing with was far too agonizing and far too excruciating for the desired comfort we so desperately needed. For the moment, we had to bear the pain in our hearts alone. "Can we find a friend so faithful who will all our sorrows share?" These words, taken from the hymn "What a Friend We Have in Jesus," let us know that we were not alone in our sorrow but that Jesus would share this sorrow with us. He would bring us the comfort and solace that we so needed now and in the coming months and years.

I have no remembrance of getting dressed for the funeral or even of who drove us to the church. My only recollection of the drive is that I was numb with shock. In my mind, I wanted to very much to cry hysterically, to scream that this has got to be an outlandish nightmare that I would soon awaken from—and then all would be well with the world, and my son would be alive. While I sat in the backseat of the car with my husband by my side, I gazed out the window, trying to hold it together for myself and for those who were also mourning over this senseless death of a young man and soldier. I reasoned that I must remain strong for those around me. If I could bring a measure of comfort to others, then would I also not be comforted by them? Would we be able to comfort one another? I did not know the answers. I could not think straight; my mind was a whirlwind of thoughts that I could not control. All I knew in my mind and heart was that my dear, beloved son Bryon was dead and that I was riding in a car that was taking my husband and me to his funeral.

"What was the meaning of it all?" I asked myself. I did not understand, nor could I figure out any of the events that had taken place in the last four days. I wanted to scream at Bryon for not being more careful, for breaking the hearts of all those who loved him so deeply. My chest felt as though someone had reached inside and ripped out my heart, leaving me with a large gaping and bleeding hole. The physical and emotional pain that I felt were indescribable. Again, in my mind, I screamed at God, "This is all nonsense, this is all madness! God, where were you when Bryon needed you? You could have protected him from that horrible accident—the accident that killed him. Why didn't you?!"

There was only silence—no response from the God that I trusted. I waited in silence in my grief and pain. Then I finally prayed and asked God, "Hear my prayer, O Lord, listen to my cry for help; be not deaf to my weeping." — Proverbs 39:12

Chapter 9
Military Funeral

"And God will wipe away every tear from their eyes; there shall be no more death, nor sorrow, nor crying. There shall be no more pain, for the former things have passed away."
— Revelation 21:4

A death had occurred—and we could not escape the finality of it. I stroked my son's hair, kissed him on his forehead, and left a small tear on his cheek. "Goodbye, Bryon," I whispered. "Until we meet again in heaven."

September 3, 1993: Roger and I arrived at the church forty-five minutes before the funeral service. As I stepped out of the car, I not only noticed a large number of cars in the parking lot but became aware of the black hearse that was parked in front of the church. As soon as I saw the hearse that would carry Bryon's body, I became lightheaded and felt as though I would faint. My legs became so weak that I did not know if they would hold me up. Fortunately, my husband sensed my predicament and offered me his arm to steady and assist me. For me to have seen that hearse was no doubt the beginning of the reality of my son's death setting in. Bryon's first ride in the back of the black hearse would be to the church for his military funeral service. His final ride would be to the cemetery, so it was no surprise that I felt lightheaded and weak.

With my arm through Roger's arm for support, we walked with slow and laboring steps. Neither of us wanted to go through those church doors. We entered the church, and as we looked around, we saw a gathering of people standing in line to pay their last respects to Bryon. At that moment, I caught a glimpse of the casket in front of the church. My heart pounded, my hands became clammy, and my impulse was that I wanted to, without delay, escape from the church. I desperately needed to get away from the horrible nightmare of my son's funeral. At that moment of wanting to make a hurried exit, a representative from the funeral home approached Roger and me and quickly escorted us to where family members were gathered together in an adjoining room.

I have no clear recollection of what the funeral director communicated to us. What I do remember, though, was being escorted with Roger and Bruce to the front of the church where Bryon's body lay. I remember that the walk down the aisle was laborious and painful. I saw the people as they sat in the pews; I saw them as they wept and as they wiped away their tears of sorrow. I saw them as they watched the three of us walk to the front of the church. I saw the people, and I wanted to feel their compassion and their sympathy, but I could not. I was devoid of any emotion or feeling. I could not weep. I walked a solitary walk beside my husband and my son toward the casket. "When will this nightmare end for us?" I thought. "How much pain and anguish can we all endure? Surely we will all awaken soon, and Bryon will be with us, and we can go on as a family with normal activities and our dreams for the future." But my heart knew that this would not be. A death had occurred—and we could not escape the finality of it.

I stood there at the casket and looked attentively at my son. I wanted to memorize everything about Bryon and how he looked. I wanted to remember his face, his red hair, the beret that he was holding in his great big hands, his army uniform with his medals pinned to his chest. His eyes were closed, so I could not see his beautiful hazel eyes. I wanted him to wake up so I could see those eyes. I wanted to look into them and tell him one more time how much I loved him and how proud I was of him—to tell him how proud his dad and his brother were of him. But there would be no words spoken today, *no words that Bryon would ever hear again.* We could speak the words to him, but he would not hear them. I wanted to, just one more time, hold close this son of mine. My heart was broken, and I could not comprehend nor fathom my life without my precious son. All too soon, it seemed, it was time for us to leave Bryon and walk back up the aisle to family members who awaited. I stroked my son's hair, kissed him on his forehead, and left a small tear on his cheek. "Goodbye, Bryon," I whispered. "Until we meet again in heaven."

"And God shall wipe away all tears from their eyes; and there shall be no more death, neither sorrow, nor crying, neither shall there be any more pain; for the former things are passed away." — Revelation 21:4.

I have tried to remember the funeral and what transpired, but much of it is so vague and hazy. As Roger and I sat in the church pew up in front of the church, our young foster son, Steven, came and crawled up onto my lap. He nestled there, and I held him ever so close. I recall the senior pastor who preached the sermon, but I have forgotten the words that were spoken. I have forgotten the words of the youth pastor who spoke about Bryon and Bruce in their youth at the church we attended; a lovely song was sung, but those words are also long forgotten.

What I recollect about the funeral is how proud I was to be a part of a military family. My son Bruce stood at attention beside his brother as the guardian of the casket. The soldiers from Fort Bragg sat in the front of the church near Bryon's casket. They were all there to bring the respect and veneration that was due to their fallen comrade. Bruce, your dad and I were so proud that you were able to stand at attention during the entire service, you never wavered nor faltered. For Bruce, being the guardian of his brother's casket was one of the greatest compliments and accolades he could have undertaken for his deceased brother, and he did it with intense love and reverence.

The drive to the cemetery was long and difficult. I was physically and emotionally exhausted and did not know what to expect at the gravesite. Once there, Roger and I were escorted to a sheltered tent where we could sit down. The pastor then delivered his final remarks to the individuals who attended the graveside service. Below is a summation of the events that transpired next, as told by Tim:

"It was at this juncture that the soldiers did the military honors of saluting Bryon; taps was being played off in the distance, and a twenty-one gun salute by the seven soldiers from Fort Bragg fired three times—also off in the distance. The flag was folded in a thirteen-fold and handed over to me by the army NCO in charge. Salutes were exchanged. I then marched over to where Roger and Kathy were seated, and the flag was presented to Bryon's mother. I said the following words to Roger and Kathy and then stepped back and saluted: 'This flag is presented on behalf of a grateful nation and the United States Army as a token of appreciation for your loved one's honorable and faithful service.'"

Everyone was then dismissed to go back to the church for a prepared lunch. Before leaving the cemetery, I have one vivid recollection of a friend who came over to me sobbing and she said to me over and over how she loved me and that she was so sorry for the death of my son. What I recalled most about that incident was that I just stared at my friend with no feeling of any kind. I had simply stared at her, devoid of any kind of emotion whatsoever. I just did not know what to do. For me *the tears have yet to come.*

The flag that was folded and presented to Bryon's parents, September 3, 1993

Chapter 10
The U.S. Army Transport Truck Arrived

"In this you greatly rejoice, though now for a little while you may have had to suffer grief in all kinds of trials."
— 1 Peter 1:6

"Go ahead and place my young son's belongings on the cold, hard concrete floor that has no feeling," I told the transport's drivers—because whether I wanted to admit it or not, that was how I was feeling at the moment: cold, hard, and without feelings.

It was about a month after Bryon's death and funeral, maybe September or October, that I stood staring out of my kitchen window. It was a beautiful day, but I scarcely noticed the colorful signs of fall in the small Minnesota town where I lived. If I were not so preoccupied with nervousness and apprehension, I would certainly have noticed the leaves on our large maple tree in the front yard turning their fiery colors of red, yellow, and orange. I might even have taken notice of the little orange and black boxelder bugs, normally a nuisance, sunbathing on the southernmost side of our house, soaking up the warm rays from the sun.

But for me, this picturesque fall day had nothing to offer but hopelessness and despair. I thought to myself, "Will I ever see the beauty of God's creation as I once did? Will I ever know joy instead of the pain that is in my heart at this moment?" I silently prayed, "Lord, I believe, help thou mine unbelief." — Mark 9:24

I was brought back to reality as a U.S. Army transport truck from Fort Bragg, North Carolina, rumbled onto our home's driveway. As I watched the large, bulky truck back up to the garage, I began to feel weak and light-headed. My heart pounded intensely, and I could scarcely breathe. I could not move. I was in a dreamlike state and thought to myself, "Please, this cannot be happening to me." I wanted to scream to the transport drivers, "Go back to Fort Bragg where you belong. Go back; I don't want you here, nor do I want you to touch my son's belongings."

I doubted the drivers even realized that they were bringing finality to the death of my son, Bryon. Then I thought to myself, "Go ahead and place my young son's belongings on the cold, hard concrete floor that has no feeling." Because whether I wanted to admit it or not, that was how I was feeling at the moment: cold, hard, and without feelings.

So, from my post at the kitchen window, I continued to watch as two young drivers opened the large, heavy doors of the delivery truck and began to unload the containers. I sensed that they were in a hurry to get to their next destination, that they had more deliveries that needed to be made. Of course, these young men had no idea that I was a mother in grief and that I was watching them closely as they unloaded my deceased son's personal effects. My heart was saddened that I could not speak to them about my son Bryon and how he died. But they were strangers, and I could not share my deep pain with them.

"Please, God," I prayed. "Help me. I cannot go out into that garage where Bryon's belongings lie on that cold, hard concrete." The Lord heard my prayer and provided an answer almost immediately. My sister, Wendy, who was with me, noticed my anxiety and nervousness, took me by the hand, and gently led me to a kitchen chair, and sat me down.

"I will go to the garage," she said calmly and started to bring in the containers.

Chapter 11
The Containers

"Hope deferred makes the heart sick; but when dreams come true at last, there is life and joy.
—Proverbs 13:12

I clutched, smelled, and cried over all of Bryon's belongings. I cried for the man that my son had become and the man that I scarcely knew. I cried for Bryon, who was proud to be a soldier and serve his country in the U.S. Army.

As I looked around our living room and at the containers, I simply did not know where to begin. "How am I to choose which container to open first?" I whispered to myself. I was completely overwhelmed with emotion and indecisiveness. Once again, my sister came to my rescue.

"I will mark the containers numerically, and then we will begin with number one," Wendy said. A simple solution but not so simple for me. Since Bryon's death, for me, there had been no easy solutions or decisions. Decisions that once took me seconds or minutes were now a tremendous difficulty and caused me a lot of frustration and nervousness.

So, together we began to open the containers. Each one brought more and more tears for the son I did not know as a soldier at Fort Bragg. Each item that I found, I held close to my heart: his clothes, his books, his dog tags, his army commendations—every part of him. I clutched, smelled, and cried over all of his belongings. I cried for the man Bryon had become—and the man that I scarcely knew. I cried at how proud Bryon was to be a soldier and serve his country in the U.S. Army. I was proud to be the mother of this young man and soldier. I was proud that I was presented with the U.S. flag at Bryon's funeral.

My heart was broken needlessly at the senseless loss of my son's young life. And as I cried my tears, I was saddened that I did not comprehend the ways of God and why I had to suffer this tragic loss of death. I did not understand, but in the midst of my intense pain and hopelessness, I decided to trust God. I would trust God in that "while my weeping may endure for a night, He will bring joy to me in the morning." — Psalm 30:5

As I opened the last container, a small black notebook laid on the very top.

Chapter 12

The Small Black Notebook

"He heals the brokenhearted and binds up their wounds."
— Psalm 147:3

I was taken aback when I found that the pages inside were blank. Blank, white pages. "How can this be?!" I screamed. There was nothing inside the black book that would ever reveal to me a glimpse into the life of my son as a young man and a soldier.

I tenderly picked up the small black notebook that laid on the top of the last container and held it close to my heart. I wanted to savor this moment and to ponder what mysteries might be revealed about my son between the pages. What did Bryon use the notebook for? Was it a diary, or was it used as part of his military duties? Without warning, uncontrollable sobs came from deep within my soul. "Please, Lord," I prayed. "Help me to bear up under the pain of losing my son, give me the strength and the courage I need to open the notebook that I have found."

Finally, I was compelled to open the notebook. I proceeded nervously and cautiously as I opened to the first page. I was taken aback when I found that the pages inside were blank. Blank, white pages. "How can this be?!" I screamed. There was nothing inside the black book that would ever reveal to me a glimpse into the life of my son as a young man and a soldier. "Why, God, why?" I pleaded. "Why are the pages left blank? Why did my son not write something—anything—on those pages to help me understand more of him?" No answer, only silence. Merely more and more unanswered questions. I yearned for Bryon's words on those pages, to see his handwriting, to feel his heart. The pain of losing my son so suddenly was almost too much for me to bear, and now this final blow: no words inside the notebook that might have helped to ease the pain in my heart.

With a troubled heart, I placed the small black notebook back in the box and closed the lid. Only time would tell if I would ever again open the box with Bryon's blank notebook inside. Would I open my heart to God's healing or would my heart be closed forever? For reasons unbeknownst to me at the time, the small black notebook caught my attention, and I could not stop thinking about those blank white pages. It would not be until several months later that I would embark on a faith walk with God that would ultimately bring the healing I so desired. "He (the Lord) heals the brokenhearted and binds up their wounds." — Psalm 147:3.

Bryon's small black notebook

Chapter 13
Bryon, the Soldier

*"Show respect to everyone, love the family
of believers, fear God . . ."*
— 1 Peter 2:17a

Hot tears fell down my cheeks, and I was full of pride as I read the many comments from the commanding officers at Fort Bragg.

Bryon was a committed soldier who loved the discipline and action of the military. Bryon constantly went above and beyond what was expected of him. He faithfully gave his all to the military, and his final gift was that he gave his life while in service to his country. Bryon was a paratrooper and had made fifteen jumps from a military aircraft. His goal was to make more jumps than his dad, who had made over twenty jumps while in the army at Fort Bragg from 1967 to 1969. I like to think that Bryon made his final jump on August 29, 1993, from his car right into the waiting arms of Jesus.

Bryon received the Army Commendation Medal posthumously on September 1, 1993. The commendation reads as follows:

> To: Specialist Bryon A. Allen, Psychological Operations Dissemination Battalion (Airborne)
>
> For: Meritorious service while performing as Print Company Armorer and Supply Clerk. Throughout his assignment in Print Company, Specialist Allen made outstanding contributions significant to accomplishing the unit's mission. Specialist Allen's initiative, selfless service, and devotion to duty reflect great credit upon himself, the unit, and the United States Army.

Hot tears fell down my cheeks, and I was filled with pride as I read the many comments from the commanding officers at Fort Bragg, North Carolina. Comments such as:

- "Bryon was an excellent soldier who performed all his duties in a very professional manner. His direct supervisors valued him as a competent worker, close friend, and trusted individual."
- "Bryon was liked and respected by everyone in the command. His quiet demeanor and caring attitude made dealing with him enjoyable."
- "Bryon's mature conduct and staunch professionalism said a lot about the manner in which he was raised and reflected great credit upon his parents."
- "Bryon was a superb soldier. He will be missed by everyone at Fort Bragg."
- "Bryon was a fine soldier in every sense of the word."

Bryon A. Allen, 1991

Chapter 14
Bryon, the Person

"Train up a child in the way he should go, and when he is old, he will not depart from it."
— Proverbs 22:6

Bryon had the strongest and biggest hands around. He left no hand uncrushed and had an uncanny way of talking you into getting your hands crushed again . . . and again.

Bryon was a committed Christian and a follower of Jesus Christ. He confirmed his faith in Christ by being baptized in water when he was eighteen. Because I also have faith in Jesus, I have hope and assurance that one day, I will be reunited with Bryon in heaven. "After that, we who are still alive and are left will be caught up together with them in the clouds to meet the Lord in the air." — 1 Thessalonians 4:17

Below are a number of comments from individuals (you know who you are) who knew and loved Bryon:

- "Bryon was a big strong kid, but he had a gentle giant heart."
- "Bryon had a humorous nature and a dry sense of humor; he was a prankster for sure."
- "Bryon had the strongest and biggest hands around. He left no hand uncrushed and had an uncanny way of talking you into getting your hands crushed again . . . and again."
- "Bryon was calm, gentle, loving, patient, kind, and quiet, yet teasing; he was considerate and a role model in every sense of the word."
- "Bryon touched a lot of lives before God called him home."
- "Bryon cared about people first, before himself. He will always have a place in my heart."

- "Bryon was a hard worker and a team player, on and off the field."
- "Bryon loved God and family."
- "Bryon was polite and respectful."
- "Bryon was reserved, gentile, and had an intelligence you could see in his eyes.
- "Bryon was *proud* to wear the military uniform."
- "Bryon's red hair showed spirit."
- "Mischievous half-smile right before lovingly pinching the cheeks of his nieces and nephews."
- "I feel a great sadness and loss now that Bryon has passed away."
- "I am grieving along with the family. It is not the same, but it is what I have to offer. I will always remember Bryon, as others will also."
- "Passion is hard to find in life, but Bryon found it in the military."

Physical Traits—Bryon:
- could "palm" a basketball;
- had very large, strong hands;
- had red hair;
- was muscular with a sturdy build; and
- had a great smile and a twinkle in his eyes.
- **Interests—Bryon:**

- esteemed the military and the disciplined life it afforded to him;
- had compassion for being a paratrooper in the army—he had made fifteen jumps before his death;
- had a great enthusiasm for hockey;
- enjoyed playing fun pranks on anyone he could catch unawares (I will share one of them at the end of the book);
- enjoyed reading (and writing) mysteries, espionage, and war stories; and
- enjoyed working out with weights and running.

Bryon's Graduation Picture - 1991

L to R: Dad, Mom, Bryon, & brother Bruce, 1991

Chapter 15
Look Out, Kathy's on a Mission

> *"May He grant your heart's desire and fulfill all your plans."*
> — Psalms 20:4

I was doggedly determined that I could finish the task of writing and completing this book. But once again, I became emotionally exhausted and wondered if I actually could finish what I had begun in my heart those many years ago.

This part of the book I have dedicated to my sister, Wendy, who understood first-hand what transpired when I decided to go on a mission for my son Bryon. And now, Wendy, it has happened again; my resolve to finish the book that I have dreamed of for so long has me determined that I cannot stop until the book is finished. I must have closure on this period of my life. I ask you then, dear sister of mine, "Does this sound like a 'Look out, Kathy's on a mission' to you?"

I envision you, Wendy, as you shake your head, smile, and contemplate to yourself. "Indeed, Kathy, I know precisely what you are about to do, and I also understand that once you start on your mission, no one can stop you."

As usual, Wendy advised me to proceed cautiously and take frequent breaks. But did I heed her advice (or have I ever)? Wendy would answer with a categorical, "No." As is the norm, I threw caution to the wind and actually believed that this time, being on a mission for Bryon, would in some way be different. I was older, more mature; wounds had healed from Bryon's death. I was doggedly determined that I could finish the task at hand: to write and complete this book. But once more, I became emotionally exhausted and wondered if I could, in fact, finish what I had begun in my heart those many years ago. I have had high expectations for the outcome of this book.

"But when writing a book, there should be high expectations, shouldn't there?" I asked myself. "If there were not high expectations, then the book would not be worth the reading." I cried out to the Lord and asked Him, "Why are you doing this to me? This is the hardest mission I have been on yet. Living Bryon's death once was hard enough, but reliving it again and again through writing has begun to take a toll on me."

The Lord spoke gently to me through His Word, *"He comforts us in all our troubles, so that we can comfort those in any trouble with the comfort we ourselves have received from God."* — 2 Corinthians 1:4

"What exactly are these "missions'?" the reader might ask. That is an excellent question. I began to ponder the same—if truth be told, what do these "missions" mean? My own conclusion was that they are, in actuality, a coping mechanism that I used to help lessen the tremendous grief and loss that I felt—that these missions were to assist me in keeping Bryon's memory alive. My assumption was that if I could focus long enough on a mission for Bryon, then that undertaking ought to help ease the ache in my heart. However, much to my and Wendy's dismay, they would often leave me emotionally exhausted and done in. These missions would take me days to recover from. I would become melancholy and disheartened in what I attempted to accomplish for my deceased son. Even if I did accomplish what I had set out to do, I was left with an emptiness deep within my heart that cannot be explained.

An example of one of the missions that I distinctly remember was the first Christmas after Bryon's death. Even though Bryon had only been gone a few months and I was in the midst of grieving, I was determined that I had to write a Christmas letter—not only write a letter but also enclose a recent picture of my son. I did not want anyone to forget him, and a picture would help them remember. So in my determination to accomplish this difficult task, I spent hours working on that Christmas letter, getting copies made of the photo of Bryon that had been taken at the Great Smokey Mountain National Park in Tennessee a year prior to his death. I wanted to write the letter despite the hurt in my heart. I was tenacious in that I wanted to keep alive my son's memory. So the Christmas letter along with the photo were sent out that year. And I believe that to this day, there are those who wonder how, in the midst of my grief, I was able to write that letter. Well, "Look out, Kathy's on a mission."

There have been numerous "Look out, Kathy's on a mission" moments throughout these many years. But my greatest mission of all was to bring to a close the book that God placed into my heart. Wendy, you have watched over me during the course of those missions. Not once were you ever critical or did you advise me to take a break. You may well have thought about it, but you never once said the words. You have listened and read many of the drafts of this book, and I am certain that you undoubtedly wept. You encouraged me and spurred me on to write my book. You will be the first to receive an autographed copy.

Wendy's Military Picture

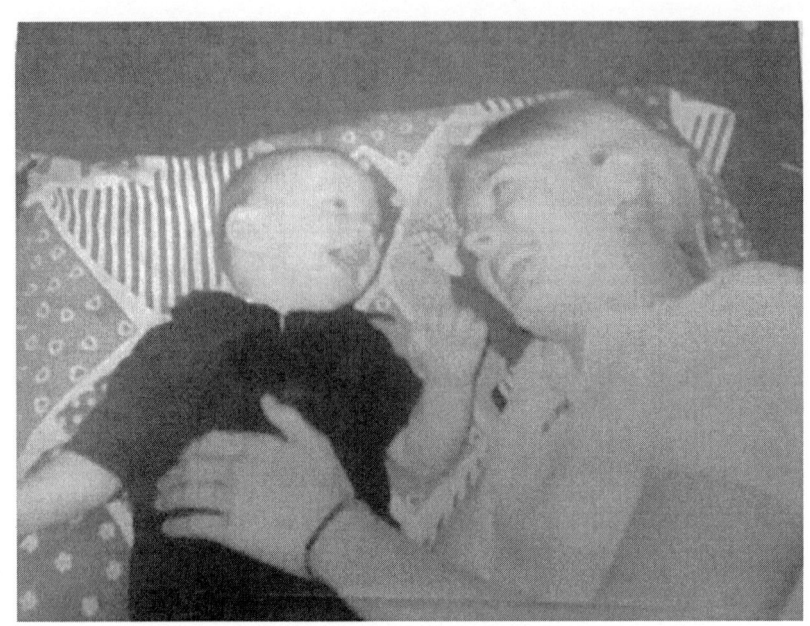

Wendy with Bryon when he was a baby

Chapter 16
That Day

By Bruce Allen, Brother of Bryon

The sergeant asked me to sit down and wait by the telephone. Then he said the most confusing words I had ever heard, "You are waiting for a phone call from your dad," and then he left the room.

August 30, 1993: It was Monday morning, officially the first day of my basic training at Fort Sill, Oklahoma. I had been in the army for nine days, but it takes that long to get everyone placed. When the army communicates to you that "basic training is eight weeks long," they forget to tell you about the first three days of processing and then the next six days of what they call "zero week." You get screamed at, yelled at, do a million push-ups and sit-ups, get up at four o'clock in the morning to run a thousand miles, and *none of it counts*! We hadn't even started yet. Can you believe that?

But back to that Monday morning, a normal military day. We were up early doing physical training (PT), but there was also an unusual day planned for the soldiers. We were going to be bused out to a CALFLEX. CALFLEX is to train artillery men for mass-indirect fires, which allows them to maneuver and destroy the enemy. We watched as the Apache helicopters, M1 Abrams, and, my favorite, the howitzers, each fired their weapons. They had M105s, M155s, M109s, and the M109 Paladin. But I was eager for the M109 Paladin because this was what I would eventually be trained to operate. We were there for one hour and then back on the bus to begin day one of our basic training.

We arrived back at the barracks and were in formation doing a roll call. I remember my drill sergeant calling my name to come to the front of the formation. My thought was, "What did I do? I am shaved, my uniform looks good, and my boots are cleaned." As I made my way to the front, I stood at parade rest in front of my drill sergeant to hear what I had done that I would have to do push-ups in front of my squad. As I stood at parade rest, someone came up to the drill sergeant and whispered in his ear. He looked at me and said, "Never mind, soldier, get back in formation."

"Drill Sergeant, yes, Drill Sergeant," I replied. The first element you learn in basic training is that the first and last thing you say is "Drill Sergeant" or the title of the person speaking to you.

I was back in formation when we were soon told to move out and sit on the bleachers next to our barracks—a time to relax a minute in between the normal rigor of basic training. We sat there for a short time and conversed quietly amongst ourselves so as not to disturb any of the drill sergeants. We certainly were not looking to give them reason to assign us more push-ups. Before long, a drill sergeant came over and called out my name again: Private Allen. "Here we go again," I thought. "What did I do?" But this time, there was something different about the drill sergeant. He did not seem unfeeling, and he did not look like he was waiting for me to make a blunder.

He asked me to follow him and took me over to the main office within the barracks. Before arriving at the main office, there was a small waiting room with a glass window. Against the window, there was a table and two chairs. On the table was a telephone. The sergeant asked me to sit down and wait by the telephone. Then he said the most confusing words I had ever heard, "You are waiting for a phone call from your dad," and then he left the room. Almost immediately, I felt a strange sensation in the pit of my stomach. My actual first thought was that my mother had died. I mean, you do not receive calls from your father in basic training—especially on day one. It just does not happen.

So I waited. I remember that it was not long because everything in the army takes forever. They coined the phrase "hurry up and wait" for a reason. Anyway, I was all alone in this little room with the window when the phone rang. I could see a group of drill sergeants outside watching me. When I answered the phone, it was my dad—and he got straight to the point. "Hi Bruce, it's your dad. *Your brother, Bryon, was killed in a car accident."* That was it, right to the point and rightfully so. This was not the time to evade the issue. I am sure there were other words spoken between my father and me that late Monday morning, but I have no memory of them.

That sentence from my dad has been forever etched in my memory: *"Your brother, Bryon, was killed in a car accident."*

After that phone call, I truly have no memory of what happened next. I was in total shock and disbelief. I could not think straight; my mind was muddled and confused. If it were not for the military personnel's assistance, I do not believe I could have made any arrangements concerning what to do next. I flew home to Minnesota on Tuesday, August 31, and was met by my parents. They looked extremely fatigued and wearied. I was in my own shock, and I did not know how to react to them. They hugged me, but there was no crying or emotion from them or from me. We were all in unspeakable shock.

Everything about that week was obscured and distorted. I could not make any sense out of the fact that my brother had been killed. I did not stay at my parents' home but rather spent those days with my best friend from high school. As expected, I attended and participated in the military funeral of my brother. I was proud that I could take part in Bryon's funeral, along with the soldiers from Fort Bragg. I still have no memory of what actually took place during those days of funeral planning—the people coming and going, the day of the funeral, the gravesite service. I was in such indescribable shock that my mind completely shut down.

I went back to basic training on the Sunday following my brother's death, exactly one week after his death. Later, one of the drill sergeants back at the base told me that there were "gentlemen's bets" on whether or not I would return. As I look back, I am glad that I did return. For someone who has not been in the military, it is hard to explain the brotherhood that you gain from the group of men that you train with, even after only nine days.

I was discharged from the army in 1996. I returned home to Minnesota and am living there today. When my brother passed away in 1993, my life was changed forever in that my brother and my friend were no longer here. We were supposed to be army buddies and share stories about that life—but that did not happen. I am married with a family, and Bryon is not here to share that with me. Bryon and I were not the same people; we had different personalities, and yet we were the same people in that we were brothers with the same genetic material. We shared the same parents, grandparents, and on down the genealogy line. My parents and I still miss Bryon to this day, and we always will.

Brother Graduation Pics: Bruce (L) 1993; Bryon (R), 1991

Chapter 17
The Leather Baseball Glove

By Roger Allen, Father

"Weeping may remain for a night, but rejoicing comes in the morning."
— Psalm 30:5

What were the chances when I opened the first container that I would find my leather baseball glove that Bryon had packed in his car? What were the chances? I nervously reached out my

hand to touch the glove. I held my hand on the glove for what seemed like an eternity, and then I picked it up.

Just as the little black notebook lay on top of Bryon's personal effects that came back from Fort Bragg, so did a leather baseball glove—a glove that belonged to me, his dad. The following narrative is my reaction and heartbreaking emotion when I found that my glove had been returned to me.

Soon after my son Bryon's death, I resumed my job as an over-the-road truck driver. It was not easy for me to leave my wife, Kathy, alone to grieve the loss of our son. Nor was it easy for me to be alone with my constant thoughts of my son, who died so tragically in a car accident in Indianapolis. And I thought of my son Bruce, who was in basic training at Fort Sill, Oklahoma. He had come home for his brother's funeral, for only six days, and then he had to return to his basic training. We were all in shock while Bruce was home—and we did not get a chance to talk about the events of the accident. Bruce did not know all of the details, only what was, in all probability, told to him by other people. Bruce was alone now as well, grieving the loss of his brother. And then, I considered our eight-year-old foster son, Steven, and what he must be going through. Even though young, he certainly looked up to his "cool dude" foster brother. I felt as though my wife, my sons, and I were alone in the pain and grief of losing our much-loved son. But the Lord reminded me that we were not alone, and then He quietly brought to my memory a hymn which I had sung in church as a child, "What a Friend We Have in Jesus." The hymn asks, "Can we find a friend so faithful who would all our sorrows share?"

I was on the road when Kathy called to inform me that Bryon's personal effects had been delivered to the house by a U.S. Army transport truck. She said that her sister, Wendy, was there with her when the transport truck arrived and that the containers had all been taken into the house. I was relieved to know that Kathy was not alone, but once again, I sensed that I had let my wife down because I had not been there to support her. I should have been there when Bryon's personal effects arrived, not only for Kathy but also for me. The guilt gnawed at me.

I could tell by the sound in my wife's voice that she had almost certainly opened those containers, but nevertheless, I asked her, "By any chance have you opened them? The containers, I mean."

"Yes," she replied, and then she broke down with uncontrollable sobs. "Maybe you should have waited until I got home?" I told her tenderly, but I did not really expect an answer from her. "I totally understand, honey, why you opened them." I then reassured her that everything would be all right. I would be home in the next couple of days, and then we could look through Bryon's personal effects together."

A few days later as I walked into our living room with Kathy, open containers were scattered throughout the room. Several items of Bryon's clothing were folded neatly on the floor. My heart pounded, and immediately, my head began to ache. I wanted to run from the room and escape the reality that my son's personal effects were right in front of me. It reminded me that my son was dead — and that he would not be coming home again. I took a deep breath and walked around the room. Which container was I supposed to look into first? Then I noticed that each container was numbered, and I asked Kathy, "Why are the containers numbered? Did they come that way?"

"No, they didn't come that way," she smiled and replied. "Wendy numbered them because I could not decide which container to open first either, so she solved the problem by numbering them."

"Good plan," I affirmed. "Because I was wondering too which container to open first."

Finally, I decided that I better get to the task at hand and opened the first container. What were the chances that when I opened the first container, I would find my leather baseball glove that Bryon had packed in his car? What were the chances? I nervously reached out my hand to touch the glove. I held my hand on the glove for what seemed like an eternity before I picked it up. First, I held it close to my heart, just held it there thinking that maybe somehow, by some miracle, I would be able to sense my son's presence—to somehow be aware of him. Gradually, I took the glove away from my heart, and slowly I began to put my hand into the glove. As I stood there, I imagined Bryon wearing that glove to play softball back at Fort Bragg. He was an excellent ballplayer. Then, wonder of wonders, I began to smile to myself. I was reminded of how it came about that Bryon took that glove, but it was a bitter-sweet memory.

Bryon's car was packed and totally full. I was talking with him and told him that I thought that his car was packed just a little too full. As we jokingly bantered back and forth, I noticed that my leather baseball glove was lying on top of his luggage in the backseat of his car. "Bryon, what is my leather baseball glove doing on top of your luggage? You did not ask me if you could take it."

Grinning sheepishly, Bryon replied, "Well, I did not think you would be using it anytime soon. I planned to join a softball team when I get back to Fort Bragg."

"Oh, so you are going to join a softball team, and you needed your dad's baseball glove?" I asked. "Yes, if that is okay with you, Dad," Bryon replied, again grinning sheepishly.

Then grinning too, I said to my son, "Go ahead, Bryon, take the glove with my blessing. Think of me when you are out on the field."

I thought to myself, "Bryon, I did not want my glove back. Really, you needed to keep it. I did not want my glove back." Large, hot tears began to roll down my cheeks— tears that I absolutely could not hold back, and soon I was sobbing uncontrollably. Kathy came over and placed her arms around me. She allowed me to cry the tears that I needed to cry. She began to cry. We cried together. We did not know it at the time, but God was collecting our every tear in His bottle. He was collecting them, and He was recording each tear. The journey of our tears and the healing of our broken hearts had only just begun.

The baseball glove that Roger found in Bryon's car.

Chapter 18
The Three Yellow Roses

"Honor your father and mother." — Matthew 19:19

"Dad told me that ladies—like you, Mom—love flowers, particularly roses. Is that true, Mom? These yellow roses are from your son, Bryon, to let you know how much I love and appreciate you." It was signed, "Love, your son, Bryon."

While on his leave from the army, Bryon and his dad decided one morning to go out together for breakfast. Bruce was in basic training at Fort Sill; otherwise, he would have been there with them. After breakfast, Bryon asked his dad where he could purchase some flowers for Mom and whether he thought that she would like to get flowers from him. (At this point in time, Bryon did not know much about womenfolk and flowers.) Needless to say, Roger told Bryon that his mother would be thrilled to receive flowers from her son and then told him the location of the nearest floral shop where he could buy them. Roger also pointed out to Bryon that roses were typically a good choice of flowers for someone special.

When I came home from work later that afternoon, there on the table was a beautiful spray of three yellow roses in a small vase. They were simply gorgeous, and I am very fond of roses. No one was in sight, so I removed the card that was nestled within the roses and read, "Dad told me that ladies—like you, Mom—love flowers, particularly roses. Is that true, Mom? These yellow roses are from your son, Bryon, to let you know how much I love and appreciate you." It was signed, "Love, your son, Bryon."

With that, I sat down at the table and cried like a baby. I was thrilled and amazed to think that Bryon had bought these lovely roses for me. This was the first time that I had gotten flowers from one of my sons when they had actually initiated it of their own volition. My husband would get me flowers on various occasions—either from him, like for our anniversary, or if it was my birthday or Mother's Day, then the flowers would be from him and my sons, Bryon, Bruce, and Steven. Later that evening, when Bryon came home from visiting a friend, he saw me standing at the table, beaming as I held up the roses that were from him. As was typical for him, he grinned sheepishly and said to me, "Is it true, Mom, that you womenfolk like flowers, especially roses?"

"Yes, that is correct, Bryon. We womenfolk do indeed like flowers and especially *yellow* roses. So now you know, Bryon that a way to a woman's heart is to buy them flowers—roses are especially nice, but in general, we women just like to receive flowers from our man." I then added, "The women say that the way to a man's heart is through his stomach." So then, Bryon, Bruce, and Steven, it is flowers for a woman and it is food for the man.

Proverbs 17:22 tells us, "A merry heart doeth good like a medicine." I hope that you were able to smile at this little tale.

Even to this day, I still cherish the yellow roses that Bryon gave to me. I cannot see a yellow rose without thinking of my beloved son.

Three Yellow Roses

Chapter 19
The Grieving Blanket

"For no one is cast off by the Lord forever. Though He brings grief, He will show compassion, so great is his unfailing love. For He does not willingly bring affliction or grief to anyone."
—Lamentations 3:31-33

There is not a way to explain to the reader, unless you have experienced such a similar horrific shock yourself, what it is like to constantly think about the very incident you do not want to think about. You have no control over it. You struggle, and you attempt to think other thoughts—but it just does not happen.

    I prayed relentlessly. I asked the Lord to please help me not continually think about Bryon's tragic death. "Lord, what can I do to stop these incessant thoughts of how my son died, thoughts of hearing about his death on the radio, thoughts of his military funeral, thoughts that I will never again see my son?" The sorrow and anguish that I felt, not only in my heart but in my mind, were about to drive me to the brink of madness. No matter how hard I tried, my mind would not shut down. I constantly ruminated about all the what-ifs that surrounded my son's death. If only he had been more careful driving. If only he had not packed his car so full. If only I had prayed more for his safe return to Fort Bragg. If only . . . if only. On and on and on my mind went.

    Finally, in desperation and after much prayer, I decided that I would crochet a blanket. Choosing the color for the blanket and a pattern that could easily be followed were the first steps that helped me to move forward to think about something other than the constant pain in my mind and in my heart.

    There is not a way to explain to the reader, unless you have experienced such a similar horrific shock yourself, what it is like to constantly think about the very incident you do not want to think about. You have no control over it. You try and try to think other thoughts, but it just does not happen. My son was tragically killed, and my mind would not let me think about anything else. I wanted to wake up from the horrible nightmare. Yet, I woke up each day with the reality that my son was really dead—and I was left to deal with the pain.

As I began to crochet the blanket, I found that I had to give careful attention to the details of the pattern. I had to read and follow the instructions closely, which helped me greatly in that I had to focus on the task at hand rather than focus on my grieving heart. Every day that I crocheted that blanket, I found that I was given a reprieve from my constant painful thoughts.

After nearly two months of steadily crocheting, the blanket was completed. I thought to myself, "Now what do I do with the blanket?" It was not a hard decision. I decided to give it to my sister, Wendy, who had selflessly supported me while I was grieving. As I began to wrap the blanket in tissue paper, I looked more closely, and to my dismay, I realized that there were a couple of "mistakes" that I had made while I had crocheted. At first, I was disappointed, but then I smiled to myself and thought, "This will be my grieving blanket." I made it while grief-stricken, and that was what I would tell Wendy. Not long ago, my sister returned the blanket to me. My heart has healed, and the blanket holds an exclusive place in my heart. To this day, that blanket is

lovingly referred to as "The Grieving Blanket."

The Grieving Blanket, made in 1993.

Chapter 20
My *Dream* of Writing a Book

"You read my heart like an open book and you know all the words I'm about to speak before I even start a sentence."
— Psalms 139:3, Passion Translation

The pain of again experiencing Bryon's death has been tremendously difficult for me. I not only lived through the first trauma of Bryon's death in 1993 but have relived it over and over as I penned what God wanted me to write.

A lot of years have gone by since Bryon died in that tragic automobile accident on August 29, 1993. You, the reader, may possibly ask, "What has taken place all these years?" I have to convey to you, in all honesty, that the journey of grief that I have endured has been an exceedingly long and arduous one; nevertheless, it has been a journey filled with hope as I learned to trust and lean on Jesus for my healing. At one very sad period in my grief, I reached up to Jesus for help; it was then that He took my hand and lifted me out of the pit of despair, out of the muck and mire.

"He lifted me out of the pit of despair, out from the bog and the mire, and set my feet on a hard, firm path and steadied me as I walked along." — Psalm 40:2

I have prayed and asked the Lord to help me write the book of our journey together. The pain of again experiencing Bryon's death has been tremendously difficult for me. Those occasions when I wrote were intense and therefore caused emotional exhaustion for me. As a result, I could not continue to write for a number of months. It was during these intervals that God filled me with hope, with joy, and with His peace. Through it all, I have unequivocally trusted in my God to help me put to paper the words that needed to be written.

"May the God of hope fill you with all joy and peace as you trust in Him, so that you may overflow with hope by the power of the Holy Spirit." — Romans 15:13

God has given me a plethora (my favorite word) of Bible scriptures to confirm His desire for me to continue the writing a book dedicated to Bryon's memory—and to bring glory to God my Savior and for the healing and restoration of my heart. God was not done with me yet, so I have continued to pen the words to let the reader know:

- "My heart is overflowing with a beautiful thought! I will write a lovely poem to the King, for I am as full of words as the speediest writer pouring out his story." — Psalms 45:1
- "Commit your work to the Lord, and then your plans will succeed." — Proverbs 16:3
- "You read my heart like an open book and You know all the words I'm about to speak (or write) before I even start a sentence!" — Psalm 139:3 Passion Translation
- "Let everything you say be good and helpful, so that your words will be an encouragement to those who hear them. — Ephesians 4:29
- "Then the Lord touched my mouth and said, 'See, I have put My words in your mouth.'" — Jeremiah 1:9

- "God who has called Kathy to write her book is faithful to help; God will also give assistance to Kathy to perform and complete the book." (My own amplified version of 1 Thessalonians 5:24)

Chapter 21

Through It All: God's Healing

*"I love the Lord because He hears and answers my prayers because He bends down and listens,
I will pray as long as I have breath."*
— Psalm 116:1-2

I have prayed and talked with Jesus about my grief and my pain. He has listened to me, He has heard me through my words, and He has answered me in His good time.

Through all of my grief and sorrow, I have learned to trust and lean on Jesus. "Trust in the Lord with all your heart and do not lean on your own understanding. In all your ways acknowledge Him, and He would make your paths straight" — Proverbs 3:5-6. I have prayed and talked with Jesus about my sorrow and my pain. He has listened to me, He has heard me through my words, and He has answered me in His good time.

Through the journey of my pain and sorrow, I want to give glory and honor to God, for without Him, my book would never have been written. It was God who placed such a deep desire within my heart to write the story about my son Bryon. I would like to state that "He has given me a new song to sing, of praises to our God. Now many will hear of the glorious things He did for me, and stand in awe before the Lord, and put their trust in Him." — Psalm 40:3

For the past twenty-five years, I have worked relentlessly and pressed on. One of my favorite scriptures has been Proverbs 16:3, "Commit your work to the Lord, and then your plans will succeed." Consider back in Chapter 10, when I wrote, "Go ahead and place my young son's belongings on the cold, hard concrete floor that has no feeling. Because whether I wanted to admit it or not, that was how I was feeling at the moment: cold, hard, and without feeling." What the Lord explained to me through this analogy was that when my book, *My Tears in a Bottle*, is finally completed and published, it will *bring fullness of joy, love, and praises to God for bringing life out of death.*

I am ever grateful to my husband, Roger, who emphatically walked with me through the grief journey and who encouraged me to write this book—even though he could not understand how I could write about our son's death. Thank you, my husband, for taking the time to read the drafts of the book. I appreciate the forbearance it took for you to read the words. Thank you for praying and supporting me in the most difficult journey of our marriage, the death of a son. Today the two of us co-lead a GriefShare group sponsored through our church. GriefShare is an organization to help those who are hurting from the pain of grief. Glory be to God who comforted us during our pain so that we too can now comfort and help those who are in pain.

    Bruce, you were ever patient with me when I asked you to take pictures at Bryon's gravesite. That was a very special moment for us as mother and son to come together and bring about more healing to our hearts. I pray, Bruce, that you are pleased with the book. I have confidence that it will bring the deserved honor to the memory of your brother, Bryon. Bruce, you are married to Colette, and together you have four beautiful children: Owen, Griffin, and twins Charlie and Ellie.

Bruce with his Mom at Bryon's grave site

Bruce and Colette with their children (L to R) Bruce holding Charlie; Griffin, Ellie, Owen, and Colette

Steven, you are an incredibly special man in our lives. You were only eight years old when Bryon—or Cool Dude, as you called him—died. I know that you remember and cherish the memories of your cool dude, and that there still is an ache in your heart, also. You are married to Tricia, and together you have six children: Abigail, Nathaniel, Katelynn, Makenna, Mavrick, and Paislee.

Steven and Tricia with their six beautiful children
(L to R) Tricia, Makenna, Mavrick, Katelynn
Nathaniel, Abigail, Steven holding Paislee

Chapter 22
Jerky, Anyone

As I turned to look, Bryon held up the bag that said "Doggy Jerky" on the label and had a great big smile on his face that said, "Got-cha again, Mom."

Remember back in Chapter 14 when I revealed that Bryon was a prankster and that I would share a story? Here is the story:

A look of disgust came across my face as I read "Doggy Jerky" on the bag my son, Bryon had just shown me. And he had that sly all-knowing smirk and twinkle in his eye that told me that I had once again been the victim of another one of his pranks.

A few minutes earlier, Bryon and I had climbed into the old red work truck to do a little yard work at our place of business. Because I had wanted to enjoy the last few remaining crisp fall days, I had volunteered to lend a hand. As we were about to leave, Bryon asked me if I would like a slice of jerky. Thinking I could use the extra energy for the work ahead, I willingly took a piece and began chewing with gusto.

It was not long into my chewing that Bryon tapped me on my left shoulder. As I turned to look, Bryon held up the bag that said "Doggy Jerky" on the label and had a great big smile on his face that said, "Got-cha again, Mom." Needless to say, my chewing with gusto became spitting out with gusto.

I enjoyed this prank Bryon played on me, and I smile each time I tell the "Jerky, Anyone" caper. And so I say thank you to be my beloved Bryon for the memory of fun and laughter.

Here is an extra short quip from Bryon's brother, Bruce. Bruce related to me that his big brother used to execute different wrestling moves on him in their bedroom upstairs. Bruce stated that one day, as his brother was performing a wrestling suplex on him on the bed, Bryon fell between the wall and the bed and got himself wedged. Rather than help his brother get out of that uncomfortable position, Bruce pummeled on him for five minutes and then ran out of the house to hide until I came home from work. Bryon was strong, and Bruce did not want him to find him. Bruce stated, "It was great! It was not often that I got the upper hold on my big strong brother." And I am amazed at what a mother can learn even years later about her sons and their mischief. I never knew that that incident had happened until Bruce wrote about it. That episode made this mom smile.

Brothers together, Bruce (L) and Bryon (R)

Chapter 23
What We Have Lost

"Good people pass away; the godly often die before their time. But one seems to care or wonder why. No one seems to understand that God is protecting them from the evil to come."
— Isaiah 57:1-2

As a family, we have lost a great deal. I can only look backward in time at what we have lost. When Bryon died, our memories were brought

to a culmination—we have no new memories involving Bryon.

This is a hard chapter to write because my book has focused primarily on the grief and healing journey after my son's death. As a family, we have lost a great deal. I can only look backward in time at what we have lost. When Bryon died, our memories were brought to a culmination—we have no new memories involving Bryon. That is why it is important for us to listen to individuals who may have lost a loved one through death. All they have left are memories. An old adage states, "When a loved one dies, we have *lost the past, the present, and the future.*" That statement is precisely right on track.

When Bryon died, we lost the past in that now there are only longstanding memories of the past. Good memories of Bryon the person. We remember that he lived life to the fullest. He really had a wry sense of humor (he enjoyed "The Far Side" witticisms). He had hands that were so large that he could palm a basketball, and we know that he enjoyed pranks and, consequently, we will no longer be his victims. He loved to pinch the cheeks of his nieces and nephews. He was kind and considerate and responsible. Bruce once told me that because Bryon never started any trouble or mischief (or maybe just never got caught), in comparison, whatever Bruce did, even if minor offenses, indubitably got him into trouble with his parents.

When Bryon died, we *lost the present,* meaning that Bryon is not physically here with us. We will not see him again, talk with him, or hear his voice. He is absent from us. We cannot invite him to our barbecues that he loved so much—he is not here. We do not have to anticipate being a victim of one of his pranks and we miss that. We cannot invite him to any family events because he is not here with us. We still miss his presence.

We have *lost our future* with Bryon in that we do not know what he would have become. We do not know whether or not he would have had a future career in the military, whether he would have married, whether or not he would have had children and given us more grandchildren. We will never know what our Bryon would have become as an adult.

Partial family photo taken 1997. Steven, Bruce, Kathy, Roger(As you can see, Bryon is not with us.)

Chapter 24
GriefShare Ministry

"God is our refuge and strength, an ever-present help in trouble. Therefore we will not fear, though the earth give way and the mountains fall into the heart of the sea."
— Psalms 46:1-2

GriefShare is a grief recovery support group where grieving persons can find the comfort and healing that they need when they have suffered the loss of a loved one. My husband, Roger, and I co-lead a GriefShare ministry through our church, which meets weekly for thirteen weeks. There is a workbook, "Your Journey from Mourning to Joy," and a short video that is shown weekly, and then there is discussion around the video. We have been involved now for over two years. Since Bryon died, Roger and I both felt the call from God to console those who are grieving the death of a loved one and are in need of comfort.

As the scripture states, "God comforts us in all our troubles so that we can comfort others. When others are troubled, we will be able to give them the same comfort God has given us. — 2 Corinthians 1:4

We found through our own grief that very soon after the funeral, generally, people return to their daily routines. They, of course, have their own lives to lead and want to get back to the business of living. They do not understand the integral, longstanding impact that is caused by the death of a child, spouse, sibling, grandparent, or a close friend. The one who is mourning will have need of ongoing support and encouragement, lasting months or possibly even years. Roger and I understand the impact that death has on a grief-stricken individual. Another understanding we gained from going to GriefShare is that we do not "move on," but we "move forward." We have learned that we need to work through grief to start to "move forward" and grieve. It is a difficult journey.

Co-leading the GriefShare group has brought further personal healing to both Roger and me. Even though our son had been deceased for twenty-six years when we began GriefShare, we both still had buried painful memories and hurts hidden within our hearts. It was through the thirteen-week course that, as we began to share our story of Bryon's death with others in the group, God began to heal those deep-rooted and repressed wounds. Our own tears of grief from the past and the brand-new tears within the group were the beginning of mending old wounds for us and the beginning of mending of new wounds for those who were grieving afresh.

At the beginning of this chapter, I shared Psalms 46:1-2 because that scripture has a special place in my heart. It was read at Bryon's memorial service at Fort Bragg on September 2, 1993. A videotape of our son's memorial service was sent to us several weeks after his funeral, and the entire Psalm 46 was read at his service.

I would like to address the question: *Does grief ever truly go away?* For me, the answer to that question is an unequivocal "yes." I addressed this subject of grief numerous times throughout my book. I did not always understand the ways of God, but I trusted him throughout my grief. I prayed and talked with God continually about my pain and suffering, but I never doubted the sovereignty of

God and His ways. And I wrote in my journal daily, expressing my feelings of what had taken place in my life.

Psalm 55:22 tells us to "Cast your burden on the Lord, and He shall sustain you; He shall never permit the righteous to be moved." I did cast my burden of grief on the Lord Jesus, and He sustained me. Jesus is our one true friend, and He can be depended upon to bear our burdens, whether that be in the midst of grief, pain, unhappiness, depression, or heartache. I have grieved but not as those who have no hope (1 Thessalonians 4:13). Bryon's memory lives on in my heart, and I will never forget the son that was with my family and me for twenty-plus years. I praise the Lord that I can now smile and joyfully talk about Bryon with ease. I say to you, the reader, that I would gladly read my book out loud to any person who would like me to read it to them, and that would surely bring to me fullness of joy. And, obviously, I know what the end of the book holds for me—healing of my broken and shattered heart.

"Now to Him who is able to do exceedingly abundantly according to the power that works in us." — Ephesians 3:20

For now, Roger and I know that it is God's will that we continue to co-lead GriefShare as long as God wants us to be of service to those individuals who need comfort, encouragement, and ultimate healing during the grief process of a loved one. I have included information about the nearest GriefShare in your area:

Phone: 800-395-5755 (US/Canada)
Email: info@griefsharre.org
Web: www.griefshare.org or www.churchinitiative.org

Author, Kathy, and husband, Roger

Chapter 25
What Not to Say

"Gentle words bring life and health; a deceitful tongue crushes the spirit."
—*Proverbs 15:4*

For our own comfort and relief, we want to get away from the person who is grieving rather than try to bring about comfort to them.

Ask yourself: Why do we blunder and falter when we come face-to-face with a person who is grieving the death of a loved one?

I sincerely believe in our hearts that we do recognize the need to say something that will bring comfort to the one who is sad and despondent. Instead, because of our own discomfort in the situation, we might unintentionally say hurtful and inept words. For our own comfort and relief, we want to get away from the person who is grieving rather than try to bring about comfort to them.

Below are several true phrases (and there are countless more) of *what not to say* to a person who is grieving. Yes, Roger and I have suffered under several of these well-meaning expressions:

1. "At least they were not drunk or intoxicated when they died" (in a car accident). (*In its place, say, "I am so sorry for your loss."*)
2. "I know how you feel." (*In its place, say, "I can only imagine how you are feeling."*)
3. "Others have it worse than you." (*In its place, say, "I am so sorry for the pain that you are going through."*)
4. "Aren't you over your grief yet?" (*In its place, say, "Is there anything I can do to help you through your grief?"*)
5. "Why are you still crying?" (*In its place, say, "Could I come over sometime and sit with you? Maybe you could share with me about your loved one."*)

6. Saying nothing at all. This, to me, is the worst offender of them all. Many people do not reach out because they feel uncomfortable. *(In its place, say, "Could you possibly share a memory with me of your loved one?")*
7. "At least the other twin lived." *(In its place, say, "I am sorry for the loss of one of your twins.")*
8. "Do not let the children see your sadness." *(In its place, say, "I would like to come over to see you and your children during this difficult time.")*
9. "Quit talking about them, you are making me sad." *(In its place, say, "I would love to hear more about your loved one," and be a good listener.)*
10. "God will never give you more than you can handle." *(In its place, say, "I know this is difficult for you, but your family and friends will bring encouragement to you.")*

Chapter 26
Additional Pictures

Roger with sons, Bryon (3); Bruce (1)

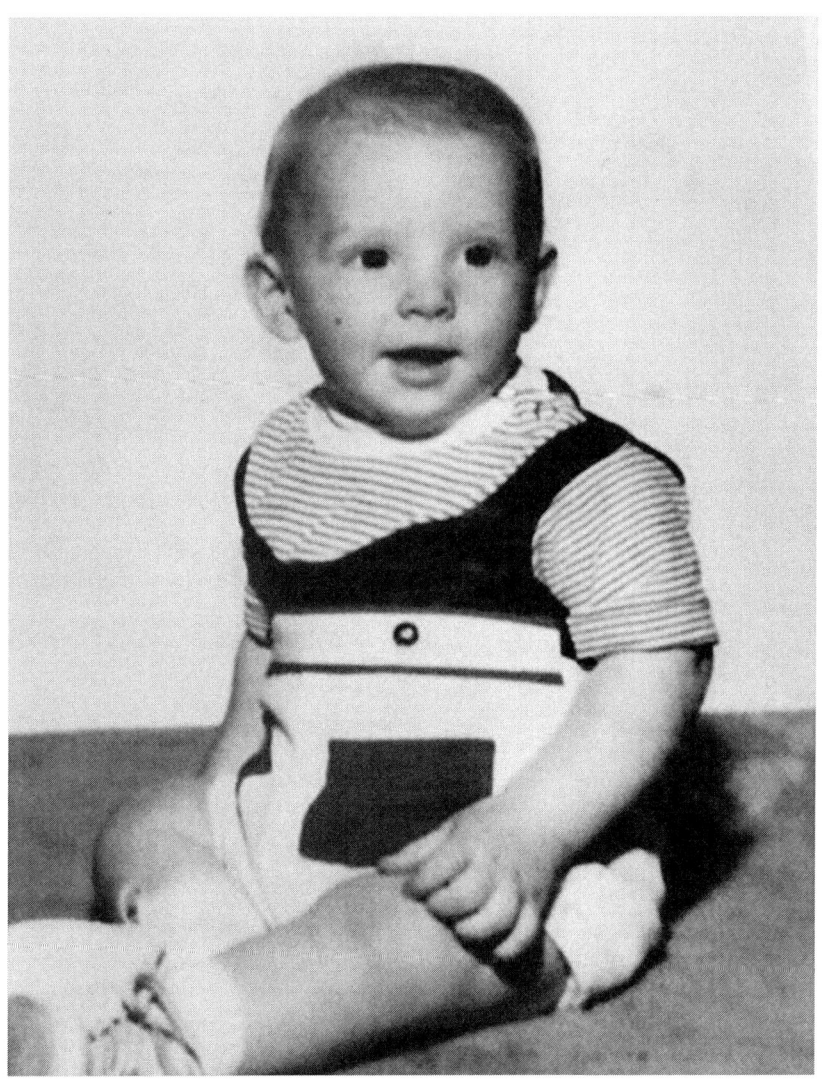

Bryon: Age eight months

Bryon: High school graduation 1991

In Memory

BRYON ALLEN
Oct. 2, 1972 — Aug. 29, 1993

We remember you, Bryon, with only the fondest of memories. It is a time for us to reflect and also a time for us to say "Thank You" to all who have been there for us during our grief.

Bryon Allen

Bryon, you live on in our hearts and we miss you more than words can express.

We Love You.
Your family,
Mom, Dad, Bruce and Steven

In Memory: Bryon A. Allen

Bryon with his dad, 1991 Fort Jackson, South Carolina

Grandpa and Grandma with their ten grandchildren

Chapter 27
My Personal Testimony

On September 2, 1979, I placed my faith and trust in Jesus Christ as my personal Savior, and I have been a faithful follower of Jesus since that time. That decision was made over forty years ago—and not once have I regretted my choice to follow Jesus. One day, I will again see Bryon, who is waiting for me in heaven with Jesus, as he was also a follower of Jesus.

The Bible offers only one step to salvation, and that is faith in Jesus as the risen Christ. Romans 10:9 presents the essential belief for salvation: "If you confess with your mouth that Jesus is Lord and believe in your heart that God raised Him from the dead, you will be saved."

This includes faith that Jesus is the Son of God and that Jesus was literally resurrected from the dead. Ephesians 2:8-9 states, "For by grace you have been saved through faith. And this is not your own doing; it is the gift of God, not a result of works, so that no one may boast."

If you are uncertain about your salvation, you can settle your doubts right now. Ask yourself: Are you willing to place your faith in Jesus Christ as your Savior and receive this free gift of eternal life? If you are willing, you can use the prayer below to accept Jesus Christ into your heart now:

"Dear Jesus, I realize that I am a sinner and could never reach heaven by my own good deeds. Right now, I place my faith in Jesus Christ as God's Son who died for my sins and rose from the dead to give me eternal life. Please forgive me of my sins and help me to live for you. Thank you for accepting me and giving me eternal life."

If you have prayed this prayer and would like to share your newfound faith, please email me at the address below, as I would like to hear from you.

kathy.allen1975@gmail.com

Tribute to service members

Thank you, Roger, Bryon, and Bruce
For your service to the
United States of America,
and thank you to all members
of the armed forces for your service.

Thank you to my husband, Roger, and my sons, Bryon & Bruce, for their service in the army.

About the Author

"Don't die with a book in your heart." God spoke these words to her twice twenty-plus years ago. God wanted her to write a book about the death of her and her husband's young son, Bryon, who had died in an automobile accident in 1993 on his way back to his base at Fort Bragg, North Carolina, after a month's leave at home. It would be a book relating to her grief, sorrow, and pain and to God's ultimate healing of her broken heart. It would describe her journey with God as she took a step of faith to write in Bryon's small, black military logbook that had come with his personal effects from Fort Bragg, North Carolina.

The story has a unique twist in the way in which she learned of her son's death in a car accident. When she found a small notebook that belonged to Bryon, the pages were blank—so she began to fill the notebook with words, especially on the days when they simply flowed out from her heart.

Her first written words in Bryon's book were particulars such as, "Where does one begin?" and "How does one begin? Will the pain ever subside? The pain of losing Bryon so suddenly is almost more than I can bear. My heart hurts, my body hurts, and my mind does not seem to function clearly."

A step of faith and her penned words in that small, black notebook were the beginning of God's healing for her. God comforted her heart with Psalms 34:17-18: "The righteous cry out, and the Lord hears them, He delivers them from all their troubles. The Lord is close to the brokenhearted, and saves those who are crushed in spirit." Another passage also provided comfort: "God comforts us in all our troubles so that we can comfort others. When others are troubled, we will be able to give them the same comfort God has given us." — 2 Corinthians 1:4

Do you suffer grief differently depending on the age or circumstances of how someone died? On the other side of that question: Does society treat you and your grief differently based on who and what happened? Does grief ever truly go away?

Kathy recounts the details of the arduous journey of grief and mourning, of sorrow and anguish, and of broken and shattered dreams. And then comes the ultimate healing of her broken heart. By detailing her own grief and healing, the book's purpose is to comfort others in their pain and grief. Now, along with her husband, Roger, she co-leads a GriefShare group in which she gives the same comfort to them as *God has given to her.*